Working with Singi...

A SACRED JOURNEY

Andrew Lyddon

POLAIR PUBLISHING
London · England
www.polairpublishing.co.uk

First published May 2007

British Library Cataloguing-in-Publication Data
A catalogue record for this book is available from the British Library

ISBN 978-1-905398-10-2

DEDICATION
*To my wife Amanda for all her love and support
and to Frank Perry, who first introduced me to singing bowls*

ACKNOWLEDGMENTS
*My thanks go to Lynda Geeves for her patience and understanding in typing the
manuscript, and to my editor, Colum Hayward, for his creative flair and support*

Set in Arepo at the Publishers
and printed in Great Britain by Cambridge University Press

CONTENTS

Chapter 1

A SACRED JOURNEY

THIS BOOK describes a journey. Anyone who has a singing bowl can use it as a part of their spiritual practice, as part of a journey on an inward path.

Like any journey, there are distances to travel, experiences to be achieved and wisdom to be gained.

*

My own journey with sound began after attending a Sacred Sound Workshop.

I had encountered singing bowls some years previously but had not found the opportunity of purchasing a bowl for myself. At the end of the workshop I saw that a number of people were trying them out. I saw a bowl—small and towards the back of the table on which they were set. I felt incredibly drawn to this bowl and picked it up. I had a feeling of instant 'connectedness'. I struck it gently with a beater and the sound, powerful and clear, shot through me.

Thinking that these bowls were only for demonstration and not for sale, I went to put the bowl back down onto the table. As I did so I had a curious sensation—it was a mixture of feelings. It was like the bowl was part of me, like a limb, and that parting from it would be like losing something precious and denying part of myself. I also had an intuition or feeling that I was meant to work with this bowl.

I turned to one of the workshop facilitators and said plaintively 'I wish this bowl was for sale' and received the reply 'actually all these bowls are for sale'. Needless to say, I purchased it immediately.

I mention this episode because it demonstrates some of the experiences that may be encountered when buying a bowl. If you are open intuitively, and it is meant to be, then you may well find that the bowl chooses you. Why should this be? Possibly because there is a particular sound that you need, a sound that will take you on your journey—like a river whose waters carry the boat-bound traveller. But the River of Sound has many aspects and you may find that you become aware of other sounds that you need, and more bowls to match these awakened needs.

An open heart and an open mind will guide you to the right sound.

What makes Singing Bowls so Special?

Although in the course of this book we will offer a number of explanations, one answer is that sound is incredibly powerful and assists in opening up new levels of inner awareness

Sound helps you explore and engage that deep wisdom within. Singing bowls are some of the best 'Sound Tools' you can use.

Practice with a singing bowl and you can start to travel, not through space, but through consciousness. Singing bowls are ritual objects (not performing instruments) and were devised and used for the practice of meditation and spiritual unfoldment.

The approach set out in this book is to consider the ritual and meditative use of singing bowls as paramount and fundamental. They are not playthings! I have therefore written extensively about appropriate dedications, invocations and mantrams for use with singing bowls. I have also included help in meditating with singing bowls, including possible meditations. Adherence to the guidance I have given is a matter of personal choice, but the guidance is there because work with singing bowls is itself a path of spiritual unfoldment—a sacred journey—and requires appropriate respect and mindfulness.

Why are Singing Bowls so Named?

If you strike a singing bowl, you will hear not only a single tone but various sounds consisting of a rich series of tones containing a strong fundamental note and series of other harmonics called 'overtones'. The profusion of overtones is beyond anything experienced with western musical instruments, if you hold the bowl in one hand and run the beater around the rim, the bowl should emit a continuous tone or vibration, often altering in pitch, which is of great beauty and power—it will 'sing'.

Strike a piano key, let us say middle C, and what you hear sounds melodic not simply because of its own tone but because there are in fact overtones manifesting which give richness and variety to the sound. However, where a piano will differ from a singing bowl is that the bowl is made to produce a far greater variety of sounds and subtleties of tone—each note on the piano is tuned to a far narrower and tighter range.

Singing bowls are in fact not tuned to a particular key. You cannot play a bowl like you would a violin, they are percussive instruments and do possess a tonal range, depending on size and metal quality, but having said this they have a function and purpose radically different from western musical instruments. It may be that a bowl will emit a note closely corresponding to our western musical scale, but if it does, this is accidental, at least for the older metal singing bowls. The tones singing bowls emit play upon the consciousness in subtle ways and act like a starting mechanism to our inner spiritual senses.

This is not to deny the beauty of sound created by such instruments as the piano, merely to point out the reason behind the effects of sound produced by the singing bowl.

Where do Singing Bowls come from?

Singing bowls came to the west from the 1970s onwards, mainly from Buddhist religious centres. One great source was Tibet, and as a consequence of the disruption and dissolution of these religious centres in that land, many bowls were sold and dispersed around the World. The context in which many of the bowls came out of Tibet was one of conflict, and none of us would endorse attacks on age-old religions. Nonetheless, we can see their arrival in the West as a blessing, because they have enriched our lives and helped to enrich our understanding of the spiritual dimensions of sound. They come to us as aids to our spiritual unfoldment.

However, bowls do not just come from Tibet. Today, singing bowls can come to us from places such as Nepal and are mostly (though not entirely) made for export. This is not to say these bowls are inferior, merely that the bulk of the older bowls of sacred origin are now dispersed, a great number of them to the West.

Their history very probably predates the advent of Buddhism in Tibet (from the fourth to eighth century CE) and goes further back in time to the practices of the Bon, who were the shamanistic people of the pre-Buddhist Tibetan and Himalayan region and whose practices were deeply magical. Over time some of these practices became absorbed into Tibetan Buddhism, although the practices of Bon have co-existed peacefully with the majority Buddhist faith.*

Although we traditionally associate singing bowls with Tibet they were, and still are, used elsewhere in the Himalayan region—for example in Nepal and Bhutan—and also further east, where bowls have been used in countries such as Japan.

*For more about the Bonpo, see glossary. A useful and popular introduction to the Bonpo may be found in Peter Mathiessen's classic book THE SNOW LEOPARD (1978).

Chapter 2

PHYSICAL AND SPIRITUAL SOUND

IT MAY be helpful at this point to explain exactly what is meant by sound, for it will help us as we move on this journey of discovery, firstly to consider physical then spiritual sound.

Physical Sound

Sound is a waveform. It moves through substance of different kinds, such as metal, wood, water and air. It is the vibration or movement of matter. With the larger singing bowls, you can actually see this vibration, and can certainly feel the vibration of any bowl you are holding. Strike a singing bowl, watch it vibrate and note that the vibration causes compression waves or movements in the air. They 'radiate' away from the bowl as sound.

As a sound wave hits an object it can cause that object to vibrate—for example, in our ear drum. As the sound enters into the inner ear it is changed into nerve signals. Sound can be felt bodily, a common experience if you stand by large hi-fi speakers, or indeed if you have a singing bowl resting on your body!

Resonance is the term we use to describe

the frequency or rate of vibration of any given object when struck. An object resonating at a certain frequency can cause another object's vibration to come into alignment with it. You may strike a bowl and the unstruck one standing by its side will begin to vibrate.

Sympathetic Resonance occurs when two bodies have similar frequencies or vibrations.

Entrainment or forced resonance occurs when a more powerful vibration hits a weaker one and causes it to synchronize and change its vibrations to the patterns of the stronger tone.

We shall consider resonance and entrainment again when we come to consider using the singing bowl for Sound Healing.

Spiritual Sound

At the spiritual level on the inner planes sound turns into light, colour and form. This is not so strange a thought. Some human beings possess synaesthesia: that is, they can see sound as colour or experience it as a taste or smell. Physically visible and quite complex patterns or forms may be created when one strings a bow across a sand-covered metal plate.

Spiritually, this process is carried much, much further and is the basis of an unknown spiritual science, now returning again to outer knowledge. More will be said about spiritual sound as we proceed on our journey through this book. However, we could note that according to this 'spiritual science' (and modern particle physics) matter is not so material as previously thought. Interpenetrating it, the spiritual scientist would say, are subtler energies or vibrations.

Esoterically, the human being is seen as a sevenfold creation, owning not just a physical body (as understood by the five senses) but subtler, non-physical 'bodies' each vibrating at a sequentially faster rate. The Universe may be divided into seven 'planes' of experience or consciousness, each of our bodies corresponding to one of these planes.

We live and move in a physical world because we have a physical body, but we exist in other worlds too and can obtain awareness of these realms if our subtle senses, and bodies, are developed. Meditation with sound is just such a way to access these realms. We noted what sound did on the physical level, but when I strike a singing bowl what happens spiritually? On the 'inner planes' the physical sound creates inner forms of light and movement.

Sound can be deeply penetrative at the inner levels. It can cause a link to be made between the everyday consciousness of our personality and the higher consciousness of our soul.

How are Singing Bowls made?

The wave of original singing bowls which swept the West is past. Most of these hand-made and deeply powerful bowls have passed into the hands of collectors. Of course collections are broken up, they can come up for sale, and there are still some old bowls on the market, but the majority now are new and not necessarily made with the same magical knowledge. This is not to say that they are bad, for there are some very good bowls available. Many of the newer bowls come from workshops in Nepal and India.

The 'ingredients' of a singing bowl can be complex. Because of the shamanistic history of the bowls it has been suggested that they were made up of sacred metals corresponding to the seven metals of the ancient astrological planets, namely:

Sun	-	gold
Moon	-	silver
Mercury	-	mercury
Venus	-	copper
Mars	-	iron
Jupiter	-	tin
Saturn	-	lead

The argument was that if one were to require a bowl which could be used for ritual or healing work that was connected to the Moon, then a greater proportion of silver would be used in the blending of the ingredients going to make up that bowl. This would give the bowl its particular resonance, tone and quality and its associations with the spiritual aspects of the colour silver.

Other opinion suggests that rather than containing an admixture of seven 'planetary metals', bowls were made from alloys that included semi-precious stones and even meteorite.

It is likely, given the fact that bowls are ritual objects, that at least in the old days they were made at dates and times which were magically and astrologically propitious—made in due time and season, we might say. Also, during the making certain mantras or chants could be said (or sung) to will the bowl into being. This would involve invocations and aligning it with the particular deity or force that the sound of the bowl was meant to express. Of course, all this would be done according to the rites and knowledge of the place and period of manufacture and, let us not forget, according to the availability of the local material. Therefore the makers would not be using western astrology or deities.

Examining old bowls, you can tell by comparing the colour and texture of the metal that different admixtures and alloys have been used. You can also tell if one metal predominates, but trying to work out if a bowl contains three, four or five planetary metals is difficult to do, unless one melted down the bowl and subjected the ingredients to metallurgical analysis, but this defeats the point of buying one!

Singing bowls can be made in broadly three ways: hand-hammering, casting, or turning on a lathe. In the first process the liquid metal would be poured onto a flat surface and after congealing would be beaten into shape. You can usually tell if a bowl has been hand-hammered by the indentations on its surface.

Another way to make a bowl would be to pour the liquid metal into a pre-made cast, allowing the bowl to cool and thereby creating a more even surface. The third way would be to place the metal on a lathe and turn it mechanically and while doing so shape the metal into the desired form and consistency. These are so-called machine-made bowls.

The old bowls I have come across have mostly been hand-hammered, though not all have overly marked indentations. I do not rule out that old makers used casting as well. The newer bowls available can be made either as hammered, cast or turned on a lathe. They are often made of 'bell-alloy'—usually a combination of copper and tin.

How do I Tell an Old Bowl from a New One?

You may well ask, 'How do I tell an old bowl from a new one?'. First, let me state some pref-erences: generally old bowls are preferable if you can find them. They have been made with spiritual knowledge, worked with over time, sometimes for hundreds of years, and have a rich and complex sound structure. Gener-ally speaking, unless they have been cleaned up, the metal will look dark and the darker the metal (usually) the older the bowl. If you look at the indentations on an old hand-ham-mered bowl they will usually look especially dark, consistent with age and usage. However, it could be possible to 'distress' a new bowl by applying say charcoal to the metal, thus mak-ing it artificially darker.

There are also many good new bowls and reputable dealers will tell you if it is old or not. Some new bowls can sound wonderful, but if the sound emitted from a bowl
—lacks complexity of tone and/or
—lacks a long 'sustain' and/or
—sounds shrill and possesses a smooth machine-like surface
the chances are it is a very new bowl and

OLD BOWL

NEW BOWL

possibly not the best you could purchase.

If you find an old bowl of good quality, it will have a sound which is complex and multi-toned, exhibiting a long sustain (i.e. when you strike it once the tone continues for some time). It is likely to have an indented and/or rough darkened surface. Of course, not every old bowl is good, but we are dealing with trends and tendencies here. You may also come across remetalled bowls. These are old or damaged ones that have been melted down again and remade, either cast or hammered.

Whether old or new, the sound is everything. Test out some bowls and be guided by the sound. Remember, the sound that you need is out there waiting for you and will call you as you select which bowl to choose.

Where to Purchase a Bowl

There are two methods of buying a bowl. One is by going to a shop or dealer, picking a bowl or bowls and trying them out. The other way is purchasing one over the Internet.

My preference would always be for going to a shop or a dealer and taking time over the purchase. Although shopping over the Internet and listening to a bowl's sound over the telephone (or via an MP3 file) might be helpful, generally you will need to handle, play and 'sense' the prospective purchase.

There are some very interesting bowls for sale over the Internet, and if you feel drawn and intuitively certain, then go with what you feel. However, the best way is to handle and play the bowl for yourself. Even if you have viewed a bowl over the web, try to get hold of it in person before you buy.

Before setting off to look for your bowl, ask for guidance and ask that the right sound, the sound that you need may come to you. Let us say that you walk into a shop and see a number of singing bowls. What next? Rather than ask for a particular type, just try out various bowls and listen for the particular sound. As you can see, this is shopping as much with your heart as with your head. In fact, leave the intellectual head-based considerations out of the process (as far as possible).

It may sound glamorous to own a crown chakra bowl but it may not be what you need. Rather than ask for a particular type, just try some out: listen for the particular sound you need. One indicator is that you get a feeling of 'closeness' or 'connectedness' as you strike the bowl. The sound may move or enthral you. Perhaps it is a sound you do not find comfortable but are still drawn to. You may need that missing quality.

Now, your bowl could be old or new, so you could ask the dealer for its provenance. It is notoriously difficult to date bowls accurately. If they are old they do not have documents or other corroborative material. For all that, ask the dealer—often new bowls will be classed as up to approximately thirty years old and old bowls before that date. Bowls may have been sourced from suppliers in say, Nepal and they may posses a number of ancient and rare (and expensive) bowls, down to recently-made pieces.

Do not forget, there are some telltale signs of age. Old bowls are usually hand-hammered, so check for indentations on the outside of the bowl that have an aged look (with colouring of darker hue).

The sound of the bowl is the right indicator of quality, but it will be rich, complex and often with a good sustain. Once struck, the note will persist for some time. A good bowl's complex harmonics will not make it sound 'tinny' or shrill/narrow in tonal range. It will be multi-layered tonally, with a beautiful fundamental note and complex overtones existing simultaneously.

Most reputable dealers sell bowls for love as well as money and will be happy to explain and explore with you any questions you have. They want you to enjoy your bowl, and hopefully, purchase with them again! Very old sacred bowls are comparatively rare and those that are available are commensurately expensive. Newer bowls predominate but can also be of good quality.

What to do after Purchasing your Bowl

In my experience, it is very helpful to perform an act, ritual or prayer ceremony after acquiring a bowl. This has many benefits, including:

—preparing or re-dedicating a bowl for practice
—discerning the nature or quality of the bowl

For you as a practitioner, such an act of consecration is psychologically helpful as you commence your sacred journey, because you are establishing in mind, heart and soul a sense of the sacred and that you are working selflessly and with love. For the bowl, we must remember that if it is new it will help greatly to commence its 'career' if it is sanctified for service. If the bowl is old, then re-dedicating it is always helpful. You become linked with its energy and become its custodian. Do remember that most old bowls have been worked with for particular reasons. For example, a bowl may be:

—linked with Buddhist deity (such as White Tara—see p. 21)

—linked with a particular chakra

—used for practices such as space-clearing

or —exorcism (very rare in the latter case).

Whatever its use, even if it is a bowl with simply a beautiful sound, blessing and consecration is very helpful. One other reason for this welcoming practice is that your bowl, like everything in the cosmos, is endowed with life and that working with it and its sound is a living process, one might say a life-renewing process.

A Spiritual View of Matter

To explain, we need to go a little deeper into the spiritual understanding of nature and sound. According to this view everything existing both animate and in-animate is alive. The mineral kingdom, including the metals and alloys from which singing bowls are made, has a consciousness.

The physical body or bodies of this kingdom (rocks, stones, crystals, metals) do not have consciousness as we understand the term and it is not in any way comparable to ours. If a term could be used we could say that the mineral realm posses 'life' but not sentience. The physical body of this kingdom exists in a 'death-like dreamless trance-like sleep'. The conscious aspect of the mineral kingdom exists in higher dimensions as a sequence of 'group-souls'.

That the mineral physical body is inert is not the point. Spiritually it has life.

One more point: according to spiritual science all physical matter, including minerals and metals, is really made up from infinitely small 'elemental' lives. These are beings possessed of no self-consciousness, and are involutionary not evolutionary, and are held coherently in place by the will of a higher being.

These elementals are vibrating at a particular rate, rhythm and speed. In our case, that which holds the tiny elemental lives of our physical body together is the will of our Higher Self (or soul). When that will withdraws, consciousness exits, dissolution supervenes and the physical elementals return to their source. We call this 'death'.

The elemental lives of the mineral kingdom are likewise held in 'coherency' by the will of the group soul or ego (existing in higher dimensions). The mineral kingdom's life cycle is subject to different cycles, rhythms and processes compared to the human. Incidentally the idea that all matter has life is called hylozoism and is an ancient idea repeatedly referred to by poets and sages.

All this is by way of saying that our humble singing bowl has life and our working with it and its sound is a living process. One might say a life renewing process. With love in our heart and respect for the mineral kingdom we are custodians of the planet not its destroyer. All matter is life and all life is sacred.

Let us again remind ourselves what the bowls can do spiritually. When you place a bowl on, say, a wooden floor and strike it, you can feel the physical sound vibrations move through the wood or other mediums including the air. However, physical sound waves have a spiritual counterpart which on the inner planes manifest as light, colour and form—beautiful form when assisted by the love-infused will of the bowl player.

We do not have to wait for the acquisition of special spiritual powers. Sound can create beautiful spiritual forms and can profoundly affect the individual at the physical level. On the spiritual levels, this sacred sound can be used by the higher intelligences to produce effects for the good of all. This is the way of 'white magic'.

This is background information to the question of blessing and consecrating our bowl. Now, armed with greater awareness, we can proceed.

To Bless and Cleanse the Bowl

A few simple rules of thumb apply when dedicating a bowl.
- —choose the right time
- —choose the right place
- —approach the blessing with the right motive.

The Right Time
Having purchased your bowl, do not necessarily rush home and dedicate it immediately. Be open to intuition—inner guidance—and you will start to develop a 'feel' for the correct time to do it.

The Right Place
When preparing to work with a singing bowl it is helpful to work with it in a sacred space. Of course, one can take a singing bowl and work elsewhere, if needed. However, for sustained and deeper work it is very helpful to set aside a room or spot that is used solely for sacred work. If you have an altar, so much the better.

As you work in this sacred space over time you will find the 'atmosphere' changes. To be precise: the use of the singing bowl plus your thoughts of love will alter the vibrations of the immediate vicinity. Regular and rhythmic work over time in one place will increase its spiritual energy and incidentally, will make it easier to move quickly into meditation (deep and sustained).

The Blessing Itself
We should understand that in one sense we are custodians of singing bowls, not owners. We may have them temporarily for the course of our life, but most bowls outlive their owner. It is good to feel privileged and responsible for what we possess.

When dedicating (or re-dedicating) a bowl I have found three things of great use: incense, visualization and invocation/prayer. Incense helps to prepare the sacred space and it is highly useful in raising one's consciousness. A whole spiritual science of incense exists in itself, discussion of which would take us away from the purpose of this book.* Suffice it to say that if you use incense to 'sense' or prepare the sacred space you are outwardly and inwardly clearing away the everyday worlds and thoughts (for a time). I find it helpful to use powdered incense burnt on a disk, but if you lack this, joss sticks will do.

After you have used the incense, if you have other previously purchased bowls, use them to create appropriate sound. If not, have some spiritual music, to your taste, which will bring a feeling of harmony to the atmosphere in the room. You may like to use some recorded singing bowl sounds.

*There is however a very useful book in the same series as this one, entitled INCENSE and written by Jennie Harding, which suggests specific blends of incense for specific purposes.

Having used the incense and lit a candle if you have one, and are prepared with sound, now visualize. For example, with closed eyes picture a powerful white light surrounding you. Feel this light growing in intensity and power—yet gently, too, for it is Love—and with deep reverence and love speak an invocation such as this (adapting it, of course, to your own spiritual beliefs):
'I see this bowl dedicated in service to the Light.
May the Sons of the Flame draw close
that they may pour forth healing and
blessing on this bowl'
Now, having said the invocation, visualize an equal-armed encircled cross ⊕ over your bowl. You may also find it helpful, if desired, to place your hands on the bowl as you say the invocation. After due time, close the ritual by simply saying 'Amen' three times or 'It is finished, the ritual is complete'. Give thanks too for the guidance, protection and blessing and the gift of the bowl. I would also recommend that at the end of the blessing or meditation

you seal your seven chakras by placing a visualized circle cross on each of them in sequence from crown to base. We shall discuss chakras in the next chapter, under 'chakra bowls' and again, with a diagram, on p. 43.

This form of dedication is a suggestion for you and is in no way prescriptive. It has worked for me, even though many of my bowls have been 'charged' previously using eastern Buddhist invocations. You could also use the re-dedication invocation outlined on page 38, but use the word 'dedicate' instead if you are blessing a recently-made bowl. You may during this process (or possibly before it) gain a sense of the bowl's use, or some spiritual form may be seen indicating the bowl's properties or powers. If you sense that a bowl has, for example, been linked to practices invoking White Tara (a deity expressive of deep understanding love) be guided and use this in your dedication.

On purchasing a bowl recently I myself 'saw' hovering over it the form of the White

Lotus and have incorporated this into its blessing.

I must now make a few important points:

By now it will be obvious to you that many bowls have already been subject to psycho-spiritual charging. Remember that the bowl's origins lie far back in time and were used by shamanistic practitioners—the Bonpo. Remember that bowls can be used to invoke and evoke qualities, forces and beings.

In our blessing we referred to 'Sons of the Flame', a term used to describe high orders of spiritual beings including those of the rank of Archangel and above and who in Themselves are guardian messengers from other planetary spheres. These beings, Angels or higher Devas stand above us and cannot be commanded but can be asked to be present at sacred acts, that presence is facilitated by 'sacred ritual'.

The 'Elementals' are however, behind man in the evolutionary scheme, they are commanded but only by thoughts of purest intent and selfless motives can they be properly con-trolled. Elementals are the informing entities making up the substance of the material and immaterial realms traditionally associated with earth, air, fire and water.

These terms not only refer to linked substances but also to psycho-spiritual states, elemental forces connected with the mind are, for example, of the order of 'fire', those connected with emotion and desire are of 'water'. In Chinese symbology we have earth, fire, water, metal and wood. Hindu and Buddhist systems speak again of *prithvi* (earth), *vayu* (air), *agni* (fire), *ap* (water) and *akasha* (ether).

I have been discursive here not to be glamorous, or to persuade readers that through owning a bowl they will gain spiritual power (for they will not); but to indicate the scope and nature of practices associated with singing bowls.

We must remember that right motive is everything and singing bowls are used to bless, uplift, heal and sanctify. We cannot err when motivated by selfless love.

Chapter 3

THE TYPES OF SINGING BOWL AND HOW TO USE THEM

SINGING bowls can be divided into different types. Here is a list, though it is by no means exhaustive:
—Chakra bowls
—Space-clearing bowls
—Ululation bowls
—Exorcism bowls
—Deity bowls
—Lingam bowls
—'Planet' bowls
and also 'Master' bowls, of which more later.

Chakra Bowls

Before we go any further, we need to discuss the 'chakras' and make brief reference to the subtle energy systems or 'bodies' of Man. We do so because those who made and used singing bowls in the past understood these things and practised with knowledge.

Underpinning the physical body is an 'etheric' or vital body which is a network of energy composed of lines of force called 'nadis'. These subtle lines of energy act as conduits between the physical body and the other 'higher bodies'.

There are seven major junction points where multiple lines of force come together, forming the principal chakras. There are other minor chakra points too, but for the sake of simplicity we will not elaborate on these any further.

To the clairvoyant, the chakras are seen as discs or 'spinning wheels' of energy (chakra is Sanskrit for spinning wheel); and they move faster or slower according to one's spiritual development. They also emit different colours and most importantly express different vibrations or tones. The term 'lotus flower' is also used when describing the chakras, this is because the wheel or energy vortex that is the chakra emits strands of energy or light from a central point or 'bud' and these resemble the petals of a lotus.

The chakras are located at seven points in the etheric body which are allied to major glands in the physical body. For example, the throat chakra is linked to the thyroid gland. The chakras are located as below, and in the diagram on p. 43.

Subtle Bodies

To complete our picture, we need to describe the subtle bodies of Man. We know of the physical and have mentioned the vital or etheric body. Next higher we have the body

---

THE CHAKRAS
Crown chakra, the 'thousand-petalled lotus'—at the top of the head
Brow chakra—at the centre of the brow above the physical eyes
Throat chakra—centrally over the throat
Heart chakra—centrally over the chest
Solar plexus chakra—over the physical solar plexus
Root chakra—over and aligned to the genitals
Base chakra—over the base of the spine.

---

of emotions, often called the astral, and then the body of the lower mind, this being the formative influence for thinking. Next comes the body of the higher mind, wherein is accessed the realm of archetypal ideas or symbols. This is also the plane where the higher self or soul is found. Then comes the body of intuition, which is the vehicle of immediate and direct spiritual awareness. The last body is that of spiritual will. It is the gateway to pure Spirit, our 'Father in Heaven'. We must be aware that when we speak of 'body' we should think more in terms of energy-system or again vibration.

Some of these 'bodies' which we possess are in each of us still awaiting proper development and are relatively quiescent. However, what we can understand is that we are vibration and each of us expresses a particular and unique tone, the perfection of which goes to contributing to the grand symphony of completed spiritual development.

We should note that our chakras have an etheric, emotional and mental aspect, and thus form those gateways from 'higher' to lower realms. Now, all this is by way of setting our subject in context, and of indicating how, by using a chakra bowl, one may become en rapport with the qualities it helps to access.

You may indeed have read about certain bowls working on the chakras. Supposing someone offered you a 'heart-chakra' bowl for sale, how do you know it is just that? In the first place we must go back to the principle of finding the sound you need—that is, right for you—first, and consider whether or not it is a chakra bowl second. Although there are bowls for sale that work with the chakras there are also many bowls recently made and in possession of lovely sounds but not otherwise charged or aligned. Much of the new stock is made from 'bell metal' and some may generate sounds which are 'emotional' or 'intellectual', and thus could be said to resonate with the principles connected with the chakras but are still not in the strictest definition of the term 'chakra bowls'.

The method I use to determine if a bowl works on a particular chakra is to take the bowl and raise it above my head, strike it and then pass it down in front of me, pausing at each of the seven major chakras to see what effect ensues, and I do this a number of times.

I know when a bowl is resonating with any one of my chakras because I get a prickly and tingling sensation in the area governed by the chakra. A heart chakra bowl, for example, will also encourage feelings of love, of deep heartfelt connectedness, of gentleness and peace.

There may be a welling up of feelings and emotions, as if feelings were being brought up to the surface. Other methods of discovery could include use of the intuition or past-life memory.

Intuition may be defined as 'direct knowledge'. If you have to think, i.e. use a cognitive sequential reasoning process to arrive at a conclusion, then you have not used intuition. Intuition is not 'guesswork' or vague 'hunch'. It is a higher spiritual sense of immediate apprehension. This is a faculty all can develop in time. For those who accept the principle of reincarnation, I would then add that it is possible you have worked with singing bowls before. In this case you would be reconnecting with past-life knowledge.

It is tempting to superimpose our western musical scale upon the chakras but this must be resisted. It would be incorrect to assume that the lowest chakra equates to the lowest note on any scale, for instance.

However, singing bowls are not usually

tuned to the western chromatic/diatonic scale, so widespread in the West—although crystal or glass bowls may be. Many cultures worldwide and in the pre-modern era in the West have used musical scales very different from our familiar and current scale.

As consciousness and cultural need have changed, so have musical scales. So you are advised to tread carefully. If it is an old bowl, it is unlikely that the maker would be aware of the note 'C' as we understand it. If a bowl sounds the note 'C', this would be coincidental. Note also that given the complex multi-tonal nature of the bowl's sound, it may be difficult to get a precise 'fix' on any note.

Approximation may be possible but exactness is unlikely. The only exceptions I can think of would be for a new metal bowl which had been tuned electronically.

Lastly, we should note that the chakras should not be selfishly stimulated through sound, and we must each of us distinguish between selfish and selfless motive.

Motive

If we are possessed of deep love and seek to project that into the world, to sound the note of Love, to encourage all that is good, lovely and heartfelt, then using a heart chakra bowl is an excellent vehicle for that purpose. However, thinking to oneself (or with the unconscious wish) 'I desire spiritual power, I will develop my sacred chakras and use the knowledge gained for myself', then using a heart chakra, or any other bowl would be wrong.

Selfless service with sound will encourage the chakras to open of their own volition and no special stimulation or concentration is needed. You will see and understand therefore the dangers involved when applying sound to the centres. Given that we are vibration, and that our bodies are vibration, they can be subject to sonic and mantric manipulation. But such over-stimulation would be like trying to force a very high voltage current through a wire unable to take the power.

The result, too, is like a burnt-out wire.

However, in fairness we can make a qualification. If a student is filled with love and has unerringly acted from the right motive using sound for the blessing and upliftment of all beings, then, and only then, he or she may be guided to work directly on the chakras. This development only occurs when certain conditions are met, such as:

—when the pupil is spiritually mature and strong enough not to abuse the knowledge imparted and has used sound selflessly and with consequent development of robust spiritual bodies

—where there is a service need indicated

—when a pupil is not seeking anything for them self, desires no recognition, reward or personal spiritual benefit

—through karmic* right.

If these conditions are fulfilled, the pupil may be granted the right so to practice, but under supervision of a spiritual teacher. This

* For a discussion of karma see glossary.

teacher could be physically incarnate or functioning in a spiritual body. If it is the latter case, the pupil will become aware intuitively of a developing contact or closeness with the teacher's 'spiritual presence' being felt. The pupil may become aware of a particular form or 'personality' adopted by the teacher and contacts this in meditation.

To sum up and clarify: in general, no direct stimulation of the sacred centres is needed. Through the individual's selflessness they unfold, and this process can be assisted through selfless use of the chakra bowl. If the time comes and there is a need, direct work on the chakras may be permitted, but this should only be undertaken under guidance and supervision.

Space Clearing

Some bowls, usually with a higher pitch, can be used to alter or cleanse a room or building. We all produce 'thought-forms' habitually and usually unconsciously and over time a particular place or space may become 'clogged up'.

As we previously noted, when talking of sacred space one of the reasons many churches, temples or mosques feel sacred is because over time, through conscious or unconscious aspirational thought and ritual, powerful forms emitting a spiritual radiation establish themselves in the subtle matter which interpenetrates the physical space.

The outcome of these bowl's sound is to effect the dispersal and dislodgement of forms which have been deemed unhelpful. Sound can be energetic and cleansing. If a place possesses a particularly dense or difficult thought-atmosphere, space-clearing bowls can bring about re-balance.

Deities

The majority of metal bowls, whether old or new, come from the Himalayan region. The old bowls were used, consecrated and dedicated to spiritual practice. They continue to carry that energy and given this may well be dedicated to a particular deity—that is, a spiritual being and a personification of a particular virtue or quality—or to a renowned teacher.

Most, but not all, old bowls have emerged from Buddhist practice. For example, within the tradition if one needed to invoke deep wisdom on the dispelling of ignorance a bowl linked to the relevant deity would be used.

In my experience, old bowls are not usually inscribed with pictures of deities, though some may possess symbolic patterning, or have a brief script in Tibetan or other relevant language. Given this, the only way to know a bowl's affinity would be to practice with it. If, over time and through using your bowl, you feel a sense of overwhelming compassionate love, your bowl may be linked to White Tara; or, of course it could be a heart chakra bowl. But we do need to exercise some caution, given that there are many bowls extant that are not so linked.

Ululation bowls

These bowls are designed, or can be used for ululation. This is the process (after the first sounding of the bowl) of shaping the mouth close-up to emit a 'wah-wah' sound. Take the mouth very close to the outer surface of the bowl and silently move your lips opening and closing your mouth. The bowl should emit a variable or undulating tone. These bowls are usually short-sided dish-shaped with sides curved.

Note—other non-specialist bowls may be amenable to ululation—practice and experiment are the watchwords here. Apart from making an interesting sound, ululation may have a purpose in the manipulation of sound in spiritual form.

Lingam and Water bowls

These are bowls whose tone can be altered by the pouring in of a small amount of water into the bottom of the bowl. By no means does every bowl have this facility and if you think your bowl is a water bowl in this way then try it and experiment. Do bear in mind that you will need the right amount of liquid, not too little and not too much, in order to achieve the correct sound. Here also we include 'fountain bowls'. When these are sounded, the liquid forms or spurts into a fountain shape in the bowl, or at the least the sound will produce definite patters on the surface of the water.

A lingam bowl will appear to have at the bottom on the inside a raised point right in the centre of the base. The lingam is an ancient symbol or device connected to the idea of the positive energetic, masculine principle.

Exorcism bowls

On this subject we will not dwell overlong. Suffice it to say that if a place or area is in the possession of a powerfully negative entity or thought-form there are practices, and bowls, to help affect dissolution and release. My understanding is that these bowls are quite rare.

Jump bowls

These are bowls which in addition to being struck, are played using the palm of the hand. If we place such a bowl on the outstretched palm and then curve the fingers and palm gently under the bowl, the bowl will emit a tone not unlike the ululation effect previously referred to. You must obviously strike the bowl first. Tones are then emitted by opening and closing the hand which rests under the bowl.

Master bowls

Treat with caution suggestions about certain bowls being linked with any particular Teacher (incarnate or discarnate) or high Lama. Such contact is not dependent on a bowl and no amount of bowl striking will bring you to your teacher.

If you are fortunate, or rather karmically granted, the gift of such a bowl, for they do exist, money will probably not change hands and you will not be seeking such a precious object. It will arrive 'accidentally' or some sign or token will indicate that you are its intended purchaser should you find such a bowl in a shop.

Such a bowl may be linked to a particular lineage or tradition (or inner plane Adept) and can generate a powerful psychological link with that path and its own particular vibration. But be careful about the appellation 'Master' when linked to bowls. It may be a term used to denote high quality (according to the seller). Be mindful that we live in a world where the term 'Master' is easily applied and easily claimed; it is a title that can even be purchased. However, a real Master is one who is selfless and who is uninterested in titles.

Incidentally, this term 'Master' carries a powerful vibration and a spiritual obligation and few are they who can claim it. We must all be careful of spiritual glamour, and we must not use this term if we have no right to it. The master soul radiates a spiritual presence which is self-evident and needs no announcement, title or proclamation.

Planet bowls

Under this heading we may include those bowls, precious and rare, which respond or vibrate to the 'stars'. Let us not forget that, anciently understood, the microcosm—man—is a reflection of and linked to the macrocosm or universe. As a way of engaging the higher consciousness and of linking with qualities encapsulated by the planets a bowl could be used, following the principles of entrainment to link up the practitioner and the higher forces.

That music and sound were intimately connected with the starry firmament was accepted by our forebears. In ancient Greece, for example, certain musical scales then in use, called modes, were said to be expressive of, say, the planet Saturn (Hypodorian Mode), or Jupiter (Hypophrygian Mode). Each planet is said to symbolize and express certain psycho-spiritual qualities. For example Saturn would represent containment discipline and focus, and a planet bowl would encourage a rapport with these qualities and those Beings representative of those qualities.

How does one discern that one is in possession of such a bowl? By practice—deep practice—with it, by developing a sensitivity to the tone of the bowl and by recording any images or symbolic associations which arise in consciousness as you play the bowl. Lastly, cultivate dispassion and free yourself from the wish to own one.

Chapter 4

HOW TO PLAY YOUR BOWL

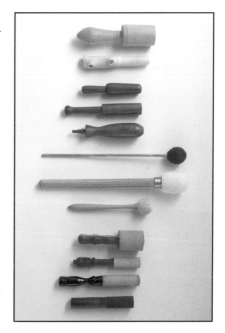

SSUMING you have now purchased your bowl, we will proceed to explore the practical issues of how to play it properly. Then some points will be covered about cleaning and care. After that we head on with our journey into deeper waters and touch upon the spiritual science of meditation and the path of *Nada Yoga*: the Yoga of Sound.

In order to play your bowl you will need a beater or stick, and they come in a variety of shapes and sizes (see photo). Broadly speaking, they can be divided into two types, soft and hard, i.e. beaters with a rope, rubber or felt covering and those which are solid wood. Their use will create softer sounding tones, e.g. with a felt beater, or harder more strident tones, using a wooden beater.

Up to a point, you can use most types on most bowls and with practice create a great range and subtlety of sound. Even with its amazing harmonic richness your bowl will still have its own limited range of sound, in the same way that one would not expect a violin to have the ability to express notes emitted by a double-bass. That said, within each bowl's range lies great harmonic complexity: a fundamental note and partials or overtones. It is this sonic openness that assists so greatly in meditation.

(i) Striking

Do not forget that a bowl's sound can alter according to where and how you strike it. There are many striking points on the surface of the bowl and the sound can also be altered by the angle of the beater as it touches the metal.

Perhaps we should not use the word 'strike' because we must not hit the bowl overly hard. To use the bowl, if right-handed, take it in your left hand and lightly tap the side near the rim with the beater. You can also have the bowl on the ground and do this. The application of the beater to different striking points, combined with how hard or softly you tap the bowl, will produce subtle variations of tones.

You can strike the bowl once and allow the harmonics to decay naturally before the next strike or strike again gently before the end of the tone, to alter, soften or diminish the sound. With some bowls you can strike and then gently wave the beater over the surface of the bowl (not touching the surface): this creates a 'wah-wah' effect.

(ii) Playing Round the Rim

Here you take the bowl in one hand and with the stick held in the other holding the beater to the edge of the rim, circle the beater round gently, picking up speed (see photograph opposite).

Start gently to move the beater around the bowl and let the sound grow in intensity. You will then be able to move the stick at a greater

the beater will vibrate and rattle uncomfortably. Ease off, and do not press so hard on the bowl. The sound will return to emitting in proper tone.

You can use both wooden or soft beaters, each will alter the harmonics of the tone emitted. The size of the beater is important. For very small bowls, I have found it helpful to hold the beater much like one would hold a

rate and the sound may increase in volume and rise in pitch. Remember, never hurry. Always be guided by the sound.

Be careful that the stick does not rattle. If this happens, it is due to the vibration of the bowl. If your stick is pressing against the bowl too hard and too quickly you will usually get a discordant or strident whining tone and/or

pencil (see photograph on previous page).

Smaller bowls need smaller and lighter sticks and larger ones heavier types. For a larger bowl and consequently larger stick, it is easier to grip the top as in the photograph below.

You can however also use the pencil-like grip on some medium size bowls (see photograph in next column), but it is best always to keep a firm grip on the beater—any looseness

and you begin to lose control of the power of the sound.

Once you have practiced and begun to master these techniques you can then move onto some refinements. We have already dealt with ululation and creating variegated sounds using the upturned palm (see Ululation and Jump bowls).

The palm of the hand can be used also to

tap the side of the bowl, if large enough, and produce a sound, you can also tap the bowl with your fingers.

Sound Tipping

This playing technique may be used with two or more suitable bowls. Take two bowls, hold one in your hand leaving the other bowl on the floor. Strike both bowls and then place

your hand-held bowl and incline it closely over the top of the floor-based bowl.

The sound should combine and produce some beautiful harmonics. But it does depend on whether you have compatible bowls and not all bowls do this successfully.

Summary

Bowls come in all sizes, from tiny ones you can hold in the palm of your hand to very large and heavy ones with diameters up to two feet across or more. By looking at the rim of the bowl you will see that it is either narrow or relatively wide and the thickness together with its size largely determines the tone. Bowls will be lower in tone the bigger they are and higher in tone the smaller they are. However, we should also add that some large bowls may produce a range of tones, some of which are comparatively high; such is the nature of their harmonic richness.

Not all beaters will work with all bowls. A tiny, high-pitched bowl will require a smaller, lighter and usually wooden beater. A large heavy bowl will only work with a correspondingly large beater. The best advice here is to experiment and use a variety of sticks with your bowl because each one will vary the quality of sound from 'metallic' to softer tones.

Care and Cleaning of your Bowl

Be very careful about using chemical cleaning agents and materials such as sand-paper, in fact do not! Bowls often have a patina to them which can contribute to the quality of the sound. Obviously over time bowls will collect dirt and dust. Regular dusting will remove fluff and such extraneous matter. If you wish to use liquid fill the bowl with warm water and a natural acidic like lemon juice (a small quantity only).

Many bowl owners do not clean their bowls, and personally I have not felt the need to clean any that I possess with liquid. Aside from outward forms of cleaning it is helpful periodically to re-charge and re-dedicate your bowl spiritually.

We have already covered this ground earlier in the book (see the section, 'What to do After Purchasing your Bowl'). You can repeat the ritual process previously outlined and then use a simple prayer, or an affirmative invocation and dedication such as this:

'In the name of the Great White Light
I see this bowl blessed and re-dedicated
into the service of brotherhood for
all humankind.

'Its lineage is pure
it radiates the Compassion of the Blessed Ones
may its blessings radiate in all directions
that all life: sentient and non-sentient
obtains enlightenment.'

If you wish, as you say this place your hands over the bowl, visualizing white light pouring through you onto the bowl. You can close the practice by sounding the OM three times. This is of course, only a suggestion. Follow your intuitive guidance and work with whatever feels right for you. However, it is always advised that at the close of your spiritual practice you seal yourself.

This can be done by visualizing a circle cross ⊕ of white light on each of the seven chakras, starting at the crown and working your way down to the base.

The Drilbu (Bell), Dorje (Sceptre) and Ting Shag

Although this book is an exploration of the singing bowl, it should also be noted that there are other devices used to create 'Sacred Sound', which have been used in the Himalayan region and have now come to the West.

The bell and the sceptre symbolize, according to Tibetan Buddhism, wisdom and method. Wisdom is intuitive understanding and method is active, energetic will. Both are necessary and when bell and sceptre are used together they reflect the harmonizing of 'feminine' and 'masculine' principles.

The bell is held in the left hand and sceptre in the right hand. They can be used in prayer or in sacred rituals. Their use can be said to help create 'sacred form in space', through the use of certain movements, uttered sounds and

of the bell and moving slowly round the edge until a continuous tone is emitted—in much the same way as one would do when playing a singing bowl. This is shown in the photograph.

Like singing bowls, when the bell and sceptre are used with esoteric knowledge they become potent psycho-spiritual devices. They have been used by Lamas in what could be described as tantric or magical practices.

The Ting Shag (pronounced ting shaw) are small meditation symbols tied together with string. They emit a powerful piercing tone and are very helpful aides in meditation. They can also be used to assist in space clearing and have potential use in sound healing.

Bell, sceptre and ting shag have been in use for many centuries and old sacredly-made devices exist as well as newer ones, which can also be very good indeed.

gestures, and of course through the playing of the bell. When a bell is played in this way it is rung. The bell can also be used by itself and played using a stick or beater. When used like this one takes the stick placing it on the rim

Chapter 5

SOUND HEALING

THIS BOOK exists as an introduction to the singing bowl and we will not go too deeply into the domain of sound healing but we shall indicate some of the general principles and activities.

If we understand ill-health as in some way a lack of harmony or balance occurring say, between the physical body (soma) and the spiritual-psychological aspect (psyche); then we should seek some method of restoring equilibrium.

We have noted through our discussion of resonance how sound may be used by the application of a stronger vibration over a weaker one, thus causing the latter to come into harmonious alignment with the former. Any discussion of spiritual healing with sound must include an awareness of the part played by the chakras, those seven subtle vortices of energy contained in the etheric body, which act as regulators and gateways between the physical and subtler realms (via the physical endocrine/ductless glands).

Through the use of correctly-applied chakra singing bowls, assistance in rebalancing one or other of the 'seven gateways' may be made. Ill-health, spiritually considered, can be thought in terms of blockage and wrong vibration of one of the chakras or a combination of them. However, and this is a very important point, at an ever deeper aspect the causes of ill-health arise at the level of the soul or higher self. This imbalance works through various realms from subtler to

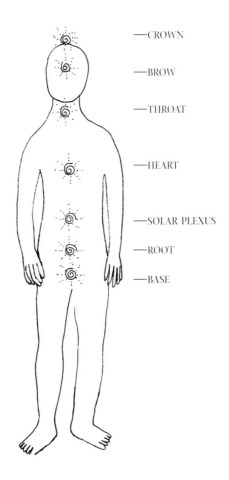

—CROWN

—BROW

—THROAT

—HEART

—SOLAR PLEXUS

—ROOT

—BASE

grosser forms manifesting into what we see as physical ill-health.

Therefore, not only does sound need to re-balance the chakras, it needs to work with the conscious active co-operation of the patient, and also at the level of the patient's soul or Higher Self. This is done by the process of establishing correct vibrational alignment. We can summarize this thus:

—all that is material is really vibration

—through correct use of the right vibration (using voice or singing bowl) dissonance may be restored to harmony in the body.

Modern science is starting to investigate the properties of physical sound waves, for example to use sound to break up unwholesome material in the body. Any use of spiritual sound-healing should be seen as a complement to other forms of treatment, and does not override the need for responsible medical advice which should always be sought.

Sound healing is in its infancy because the understanding of the subtle anatomy of Man is in its infancy. The true vibrational nature of the chakras is probably not known, especially so given that the chakras not only exist in the etheric but also in still subtler vibrational aspects, e.g. emotional and mental, and each will express its tone or sub-tone.

So it would be wrong to claim that one could re-balance say, the base chakra by sounding a singing bowl tuned to the lowest note of the chromatic scale, i.e. the note of 'C', assuming of course that a singing bowl could express that note. In any case one would need to take into account which level or aspect of the chakra needed alignment.

The reason why the true tonal nature of the human organism is not known is that knowledge of this confers great power, and we human beings are not spiritually mature enough to wield it wisely. Having said that, using the singing bowl as a healing tool can be very helpful. Generally, it can aid relaxation and promote correct alignment between the various bodies,

The sound properties could be used to break up unhelpful blockages in etheric matter, but really to work in this way probably requires in us the ability to see and hear spiritually the health aura of the patient. What is said here is not meant to discourage research or right practice. We can learn more both through exoteric science, and by spiritual methods: through humility, meditation and service, leading to developed intuition. However, we can still heal and be healed simply by playing the bowl and becoming immersed in its sound, and so it is that I offer the following discussion on meditation.

Meditation with Sound:
the Path of Nada Yoga

In this section and after, when I capitalise the 'S' in Sound, I am referring to the Sound that encompasses all things both animate and in-animate within the spiritual realm and the physical.

The Sound is that mighty word or vibration, aspects of which form the material world we are pleased to call 'reality'. To describe this Sound in essence is, paradoxically beyond words or music, it just *is*.

Approximations may be given when we utter the AUM or the OM for example. The AUM is the expression of the creative intelligence or wisdom inherent in material forms (consider the beauty of the snowflake!).

The OM is the expression of deep creative Love and assists in aligning to soul and spirit.

There is Sound behind form: the 'unstruck Sound'. There is also Sound within the form: the 'struck Sound'.

The spiritual science of Sound is the understanding, as far as possible, of the union of these two forces. When a singing bowl is struck a physical sound is made which has its counterpart in the super-physical realm. The mystical study of Sound audible and inaudible is part of the quest called 'Nada Yoga' by those in the East. Total knowledge of Sound is not humanly possible.

All creation can be considered to be vibration in a sevenfold order, the 'lowest' or slowest seventh being the physical world as known by the five senses. To know all of creation is beyond the awareness of even the wisest of souls, yet there are glimpses, and more than these through the practice of Sacred Sound meditation which is defined as:

'A meditative path having for its object discernment of the spiritual basis of all life understood as vibration'.

To attune to the so-called 'higher vibrations' and therefore gain awareness of the subtle audible worlds involves the keying up of the senses so that the faster rate of vibration of the inner worlds can be comprehended. This is done by diligent dedicated practice, fostered by spiritual selflessness, and also by using the voice and/or such devices as the singing bowl. Then, by very slow degrees, just such an inner awareness of the subtle worlds can be gained.

First comes work with audible sound. By the striking of the bowl, we are given entrance into the inner worlds; by its effects on the meditator's subtle bodies, increased sensitivity is noted. Then gradually over time and by learning to follow the struck sound of the bowl into the silence or the 'void' we become aware of the unstruck or inaudible sound (always bearing in mind that the totality of the Sound is both audible and inaudible).

Following through with the struck sound of the bowl and letting the Sound 'die', we progress to sensing its refrain reborn in the inner worlds, where it takes form as colour, and this of most beautiful hue and shape.

We trace the path of this unstruck Sound as it progresses. Let us picture this as substance of a deep blue colour gradually forming an arch or bow shape, pushing its way 'higher' into the spiritual realms. As this form gradually extends or elongates it clears a path, and in its wake creates a funnel or vacuum or void in spiritual space. It eventually touches or makes contact with the Soul, and down through this created funnel can come the guidance and communication between personality and the higher and holy realms. We have union or yoga between spirit and matter through the practice of Sound.

Through meditation, alignment and development of the subtle bodies is made. The practitioner learns to achieve focus, and subsequently is enabled to transmit or radiate loving understanding for the benefit of all beings. Needless to say the practice of Nada Yoga must be undertaken by the compassionate heart with the mind illuminated by selfless love and motive.

A Suggested Meditation using a Singing Bowl

Before giving the meditation itself, set out on page 48, it may be helpful to recap on why meditation helps and indeed works in the way it does. As indicated, when we discussed 'Nada Yoga', meditation achieves focus and alignment, and not just through sound but through any meditative practice (properly constituted). Meditation is the vehicle that takes us on our journey. It assists in proper

—alignment between physical and subtle bodies

—focus (i.e. contact with the Higher Self or soul and at advanced stages with our universal self or pure spirit)

—development of that quality called 'radiance': that is, our capacity to 'shine forth' or 'sound forth' love.

Through meditation we can give or project into the world spiritual or subtle qualities as we allow those qualities to cascade down from the very highest we can contact, down to the physical plane. In occult symbolism, this is how we truly sound our own note.

Meditation

SIT with your bowl in front of you, and before beginning to use the bowl use an invocation or prayer familiar to you. If you prefer, you can say:

'I attune myself to the Light and to the Sound of my Highest Self
I am one in the Light and in the Sound'

and then sound the OM three times.... Then pause in the silence....

When you feel guided to proceed, strike your bowl gently once, allowing the Sound full play and listening to it with eyes closed. As it fades into the Silence, be unhurried but attentive. Note any colours or forms you may see or 'feel', however fleeting. Note too any inner sounds you 'hear', bearing in mind that different 'colours' have their own tone. At all times refrain from judging or intellectualizing this process, just let it be. You can evaluate afterwards. Now go through this exercise again:

> —strike the bowl once, and then 'eyes closed'
> —let the Sound die away into Silence
> —observe and experience, do not judge.

You can strike the bowl three or seven times. After you have finished this exercise, close your meditation by saying: *'I give thanks to the Light and to the Sound'*.

Then seal yourself, if you wish. Visualize the circle cross in white light ⊕ and place it on each of the seven chakras in turn from the crown to the base. Lastly, visualize a circle of golden white light around you. Reflect on what you experienced both in the light of your spiritual practice and reasoning capacity. Allow time for any meanings to unfold for you.

Sound and Form

The exercise just given is designed to help attune you to the Sounds of the bowls and of their effects. During it, you may or may not have experienced something, even if you have not 'seen' or 'heard' do not worry, for being in the Silence that has been created by the singing bowl is a very powerful experience.

Do remember that true Silence is not just absence of Sound but is the occult retention of Sound. There is a difference; you are participating in the meaningful withdrawal of Sound to the inner levels, there to conserve power.

Another way of understanding this is by considering our speech. We talk too much (and I include myself in this!). Much of what we say lacks true spiritual value, but everything we say creates colour or form, usually half-baked and unfocused, and we fog ourselves up. What if, instead of speaking so much, we become more mindful and withdraw our speech to the inner levels and only speak with full spiritual intention behind our words? Powerful indeed would this be, and in our own way we would imitate the creative processes of God. First He–She contemplated, then spoke; and the one Word differentiated like some divine fractile of infinite subtle vibration. Thus were all things created.

Chapter 6

THE NEXT STEP

HAVING purchased and become accustomed to your first bowl, you may find that the sound which you need, and which you wish to express, expands. Thus you find yourself buying more bowls. With two or more bowls, you will be able to explore extended playing techniques.

Playing bowls becomes a sound meditation in itself. Begin by being aware of the Silence, then strike the first bowl as and when you feel guided, slowly building up the level of sounds. Then strike the second bowl and allow its sound to build up. As you do this, count silently and rhythmically—for example, up to three. Then strike the first bowl.

As you continue with this, you will find you will build up a considerable momentum.

This is a simple process, but when practised—and undertaken intuitively—it has a powerful effect.

You may also work with intervals or chords. An interval arises from the sounding of two notes simultaneously, while a chord is three or more notes. Take two beaters and then strike the two bowls together. As you progress, you will find different sound combinations, and will produce different effects, as the overtones merge with each other.

Chant

You may also want to chant with a bowl. Chanting is the vocal expression of Sound at

techniques for chanting mantrams. One very well-known technique is the Tibetan 'One Voice Chord'. This is the ability to sound a tone at both low and high pitch simultaneously. Needless to say, the cultivation of this technique takes many years of sustained practice under supervision; and I highlight these refinements to indicate the possibilities and extent of work with Sound.

However, we can work with our bowls and chant here and now.

In my practice, I have found that certain of my bowls are more amenable to chanting than others—which is as it should be, as different bowls do different types of work. Again, be guided by the Sound: the tones you need and which want to express themselves through you will make themselves known as you practise.

Having found a bowl to chant with, start playing the bowl around the rim gently and slowly. Allow yourself the time to unfold as you do this. You are in no hurry. Gentle and

a certain pitch, or pitches. Mantrams are the chanting of combinations of words or phrases which have definitive meaning. On the spiritual level some mantrams (and chants) are incredibly powerful, and when allied to the Sounds of the bowl or bowls are made doubly potent. The intensity is even more pronounced when a sacred mantram or chant is intoned with a bowl specifically made and dedicated to working with that mantram.

There are also refinements and special

purposeful is the way. Now as you feel Sound building up in the bowl, begin to chant. Start at the lowest tone you are comfortable with and gradually and gently rise in pitch until you get to the highest you can chant comfortably. Maintain this highest tone for a little and then gradually reduce the pitch again sequentially moving down the scale again until you get back to the lowest point, from which you started.

The sound of the bowl may not be able to match your progressed tone but it will provide a highly effective 'drone' or fundamental tone forming a partnership with your voice.

Some words of advice: be gentle with your larynx. Do not overstretch your voice. We must be careful not to treat these exercises as demonstrations of ego; we are not in a race or competition, and a chant 'imperfectly expressed' but filled with creative love is to be preferred above something technically advanced but empty.

Why we do this, and why we play the bowls, is to offer up sustenance to higher forces that they may use our Sound for the benefit of all life. Our journey with singing bowls can take us very far on the spiritual path. Although we should be acting selflessly, there are some individual merits to be gained through using Sound as a spiritual practice.

Making Sound as a Spiritual Practice

Through our work with the bowls, firstly we can become more aware. There is much meaning in this word, because evolution and unfoldment is a progressive series of greater and deeper awareness.

You will begin to understand that Sound has meaning, that it has a spiritual basis and that you will learn to 'hear' spiritually speaking. This is not just the development of clairaudience, which may or may not occur, but is the opening up of greater conscious contact with Higher Self or Soul.

Our soul has been likened to the 'Voice of Silence'. This is a seemingly contradictory statement. How can silence have a 'voice'?

In the emptiness or void we can detect 'soul guidance', a deep intuitive sense of direction. 'That is the way to go'. Of course we cannot guarantee that practice with a singing bowl automatically links you to your soul, but the more we practice, the more we 'listen' the greater the chances become that our Higher Self can pour down wisdom into us. This wisdom will be accompanied by a sense of peace, of love and inner certainty for the time we are able to be in contact.

Aside from this highly beneficial spiritual alignment, you may indeed become more aware inwardly of colours and sounds. I would not describe myself as clairvoyant, yet when attuned to the Sound of the singing bowls I have been helped to see the colours they emit.

Another helpful aspect to work with the singing bowl is that it helps induce calmness and greater mental clarity; but at all times and all ways we must learn to listen without ego or with the wish to acquire spiritual power, but in humility. I venture to suggest that selfless dedicated practice will draw you closer to your spiritual teacher.

We need to remember the aphorism that 'The Adept is Self-Made'. No-one is going to do our work for us. Opportunity for study or practice may be given, but after that it is up to us to work, study and do more work, with joy in our hearts of course!

Singing Bowls and the Landscape

Most of us use or work with singing bowls indoors. We have images of them being worked inside temples and other places of spiritual retreat. However, our sacred landscape (and it is indeed sacred) needs healing as well.

Esoteric or spiritual research is suggesting that much as the human body has chakras and subtle energy-systems, so does the landscape. Great cities, temples and church sites are often located on great confluences of energy or spiritual power called 'earth chakras' or sacred sites; and are connected with subtle lines of force running for hundreds of miles across the landscape, called 'ley lines'.

Just as the human organism can fall out of harmony and express dissonance and so illness, so it is with the land. I am afraid to say that as humans we have a large measure of responsibility for this. There can be blockages or imbalance in the 'ley system'. Aside from the energy of ley lines and chakras, let us not forget parts of the land upon which battles have been fought (what a though-atmosphere must be expressing itself there!); and let us again think in terms of harmony, vibration or sound.

We keep coming back to this point from different angles, but through our journeyings together we have seen how everything can be understood as vibration: our physical bodies, the landscape, even the planet as a whole. And if this is the case, then we can use sound devices like singing bowls to help restore balance to the subtle forces that permeate the land. As well as restoring balance, when present at sacred, beautiful places, one can use the singing bowl as part of a process of thanksgiving and of producing 'sonic nourishment; for the elemental and angelic kingdom.

I am not suggesting that a singing bowl will act as a 'cure-all' for the ills of the environment—but rather that developing an awareness of applied sacred sound to the landscape could be beneficial to both practitioner and the land itself.

The Future

We have journeyed together in this book, and before we part company I would like to offer a suggestion as to where this growing interest in singing bowls and Sound Meditation is heading.

I am going to assume that you, the reader,

An Outdoor Ritual

Here is a suggested exercise, for a first step in using your bowl for landscape healing. Find a beautiful and quiet space—it could be an ancient landscape temple or sacred site, wherever you live in the world (there are many in Britain) or choose a garden or piece of land that you find draws you. Choose a moment when you have it to yourself: you do not want to disturb others.

Having once selected your place, quieten your mind and ask for the presence of the 'spirit keeper' of that place. Seek permission from them to use your bowl. A site like Avebury will have a powerful, overlighting angelic being; a quiet country grove will have a delightful deva.

With your bowl begin to sound, as you do so visualize great waves of light radiating from your bowl into the air, into the ground, and directed to the tiny elemental beings of the locale. Do this for about five minutes, then pause and rest in the Silence. If you wish, repeat the process, or close with a short prayer of thanks. Do not forget to seal yourself, and root yourself solidly back on Mother Earth.

will be aware of the idea of the New Age, and that we are said to be progressing into the zodiacal Age of Aquarius. This is due to the 'precession of the equinox' when the sun is said to be located in one of the twelve signs of the zodiac for approximately two thousand three hundred years, and then move to the next sign. Allied to this zodiacal shift comes an inflow of new ideas and forms expressed to us in terms of seven rays.

If we imagine a rainbow spectrum of light it lets us see it divided into seven, each of these seven lights takes its turn in expressing some one fundamental way of being. In the previous epoch, which we are passing out of (the Age of Pisces), that way of being could be described as 'idealism and devotion'. We are moving into a period which will express the seventh ray, of ritual, ceremonial and magic. The new way of being can be described as order, rhythm and synthesis.

Working in this way gives special facility and rapport with what we shall call, loosely, the devic and elemental kingdoms (among much else). The devas respond most potently to sound.

According to the precession theory, in a very far past, men and women possessed consciously and as part of their normal equipment facilities for contacting understanding, and manipulating the elementals through Sound. This knowledge, along with much else, was withdrawn largely for two reasons:

—it was seriously abused

—the intellect was in process of development and humanity needed to understand matter and form analytically and consciously without direct access to the higher world and inner kingdoms.

Now, gradually, old knowledge is returning on a higher spiral and opportunity is again being offered, for those who can work wisely, to come into closer rapport with our loved brethren of the elemental and angelic realm.

Not only will the pervasive seventh ray of ceremonial and magic encourage this, but also due for return is another ray—the fourth ray. Ray cycles overlap and interpenetrate. This fourth ray of harmony, art and music will offer opportunity to work with spiritual knowledge and create music and sound which helps create spiritual form and then materialize it for the benefit of all life.

Sound will be seen as the vehicle through which spiritual form can live and radiate. Architecture will change as buildings will 'come alive', since they will again be understood to be forms through which spiritual forces can manifest. Much of what today passes for music, though good in its own way, is formed in the solar-plexus not the heart. What thought-forms do you think are generated by certain types of popular music? Again this is not to criticise but to set in context and to suggest that if (and this is the test) we work selflessly with love, we can then begin to become co-creators in Sound—because there are 'Sounds' extant on the inner planes, especially the buddhic or intuitional plane; sounds which are awe-inspiring but have not been permitted expression.

According to the seer Alice Bailey, the fourth ray is due to begin manifestation in approximately 2025. This is not to say that automatically like a light switching on, everything will change.

All these developments will grow gradually and also according to how they are received; but the potential is there and you can help prepare for and transform conditions. This is done through consciously understanding spiritually what Sound is, and how through your love and service you can make our world better. It may involve also the development of new (or re-learned) techniques and new musical instruments.

There are people beginning to wake up to their spiritual heritage and responsibilities, and this response is partly due to the new energies coming in.

Although I have confined myself to mentioning two of the new incoming ray energies

The Seven Planes

comprising:

Spiritual Will   one 'sub-tone'

Intuition   one 'sub-tone'

Higher Mind   one 'sub-tone'

Lower Mind   one 'sub-tone'

Emotional   one 'sub-tone'

Etheric   one 'sub-tone'

Physical   one 'sub-tone'

Each plane or sub-tone makes up one
great sevenfold Fundamental Tone

there are other rays and spiritual cycles, for example those connected with spiritual beings called Time-Spirits. However, such discussions will take us away from our path.

Humankind will also need to locate itself within a new sonic framework. Please note the table overleaf.

We noted early in this book that the human being is sevenfold: our seven 'bodies' or vehicles are really vibrations. Each plane (physical, etheric, and so on) can be understood as vibration, and would therefore express its own tonal value. The seven planes can also be understood as aspects or sub-tones of one fundamental Tone, which makes up the entire 'Grand Symphony' of Creation—as we understand it.

It would be a mistake to equate the seven notes of our current Western scale with the tones of creation. Rather, let us have in mind the great beauty and vibrational interconnectedness of all life, and think carefully about how sound can 'build bridges' beyond the veil. Finally, we could consider how such tools as singing bowls can assist us in that deeply redemptive work.

We end as we began our journey with our humble singing bowl. May it open for you a realm of beauty, truth and goodness and may you grow eternally in the Light and in the Sound.

SHORT GLOSSARY

Bon The shamanistic tradition of the Himalayan region prior to the advent of Buddhism. Buddhism entered Tibet in various waves starting in the second and fourth centuries CE, and then in the eighth century CE—with the coming of the teacher Padmasambhava.

However the practices of Bon have overlapped and coincided with Buddhism. Bon texts and folklore assert the tradition was founded by a teacher called Tonpa Shenrab Miwoche. In Bon he is given a rank equal in status to the Buddha. He transmitted a teaching called Yungdrung or Eternal Bon, which replaced previous practices cited as animistic Bon.

Miwoche is said to have lived 18,000 years ago. The practices of Bon have a major focus on the use of sound and silence. This is said to cultivate a state of spiritual openness, where a sense of peaceful oneness, clarity and unity with all life is achieved.

As well as using singing bowls, Bon practitioners (Bonpo) use a *chang* which is a cymbal with a metal clapper. This is favoured instead of the bell (*drilbu*) which is used more in Tibetan Buddhism. The chang is a ritual object used in tantric or magical rites.

Deities These can be viewed as personifications or expressions of divine virtues or the respectful devotion and inculcation of qualities exhibited by great sages and teachers. The latter could be individuals such as Manjushri/Jompal Shenyen or Padmasambhava. Both of these teachers may be said to be exponents of deep wisdom.

Karma   The process of cause leading to effect. An action, thought or word generated by a human that has its resultant effect in this life or some other future life.

Pitch   Musically understood, is the highness or lowness of tone.

Reincarnation Successive or repeated lives lived on earth powerfully influenced by karma, leading towards an opportunity to grow through joy or error.

Scale   Musically understood, a series of pitches in an ascending or descending sequence.

Time Spirits   A sequence of seven Archangelic Beings, who each take on the role successively of Spirit of the Age. They work on a three hundred-year cycle. The current reigning Time Spirit is the Archangel Michael, who is Lord of Cosmic Intelligence. Epochs conditioned by Him are marked by a high degree of cosmopolitanism. In the West He is known as 'the Countenance of Christ'.

Tone   Musically understood, is a sound struck at a specific pitch. The term can also be used to suggest sound qualities or timbre

Spiritually understood, the movement at a particular rate, rhythm or speed of the elementals comprising any specified body or vehicle of manifestation.

BIBLIOGRAPHY AND RESOURCES

Ted Andrews, SACRED SOUNDS: MAGIC AND HEALING THROUGH WORDS AND MUSIC. 2nd edition, 2003, Llewellyn Publications

Hans Cousto, THE COSMIC OCTAVE: ORIGIN OF HARMONY. Revised edition 2000, Life Rhythm Books

Jonathan Goldman, HEALING SOUNDS: THE POWER OF HARMONICS. 1992, Healing Arts press

Anneke Huyser, SINGING BOWL EXERCISES FOR PERSONAL HARMONY. 1999, Binkey Kok Publications

Eva-Rudy Jansen, SINGING BOWLS: A PRACTICAL HANDBOOK OF INSTRUCTION AND USE. 1992, Binkey Kok Publications.

As this is an introductory book, I have not given an extensive bibliography, but just provided suggestions for further reading. The books cited will in most cases have bibliographies and there are other reference sources. The following is a very useful internet resource:

www.frankperry.co.uk

Frank Perry has been working with singing bowls for forty years. His site contains expanded and comprehensive information on sacred sound. It also contains an extensive bibliography of works on the spiritual dimensions of sound.

At the time of writing, Frank is working on a book encapsulating his insights and vast experience and it is eagerly awaited.

Those interesting in purchasing my own CD recordings of the sounds of the singing bowl are directed to the following website. Follow the 'Contact' links there.

www.keystolight.co.uk